THE STUDY OF
MEDIEVAL HISTORY

THE STUDY OF
MEDIEVAL HISTORY

AN INAUGURAL LECTURE DELIVERED
ON 17 NOVEMBER 1937

by

C. W. PREVITÉ-ORTON

*Fellow of St John's College and Professor
of Medieval History in the University of
Cambridge*

CAMBRIDGE

AT THE UNIVERSITY PRESS

1937

CAMBRIDGE
UNIVERSITY PRESS

University Printing House, Cambridge CB2 8BS, United Kingdom

Published in the United States of America by Cambridge University Press, New York

Cambridge University Press is part of the University of Cambridge.

It furthers the University's mission by disseminating knowledge in the pursuit of education, learning and research at the highest international levels of excellence.

www.cambridge.org
Information on this title: www.cambridge.org/9781107644625

© Cambridge University Press 1937

First published 1937
First paperback edition 2014

A catalogue record for this publication is available from the British Library

ISBN 978-1-107-64462-5 Paperback

THE STUDY OF
MEDIEVAL HISTORY

The first holder of a new professorial chair may
well begin his inaugural lecture with some
diffidence. He has no inherited credit to sup-
port him, no robe borrowed from eminent
predecessors which may conceal his own de-
merits and give some reflected light to supply
a faint lustre to his own darkness. It is natural,
therefore, that, in this poverty of prestige, I
should recall to you that, though the chair is
new, medieval studies are no novelty in Cambridge; that they have been pursued in the
University with a zeal and effectiveness which
may well bear comparison with other disci-
plines and other centres of learning. Living
names are a forbidden theme, but there is no
embargo on citing and on praising the dead.
And of the dead there is an illustrious succession
of Cambridge men. If not all of them did their
work as residents, they had all submitted to the

training this University gave them and, we may claim, were manifestations of a Cambridge spirit of exact learning and critical enquiry. "*Hinc lucem et pocula sacra.*"

The Middle Ages were hardly done when John Leland, once of Christ's College, made those Itineraries and Collectanea which were aimed at a systematic research into the history of England "to the intent that the monuments of ancient writers, as well of other nations as of our provinces, might be brought out of cloudy darkness to lively light". He has been called "the father of English antiquaries", but his diligent survey makes him the father, too, of the mass of bibliographical, cataloguing, calendaring work which has been the laborious and indispensable adjunct of historical studies, and in which, as in so much else, the late Provost of Eton and King's has placed us immeasurably in his debt. And Leland's own date made his theme mainly medieval: the rival modern history had not yet happened; a historian who did not concentrate on ancient Greece and Rome was bound, if he did not

(6)

know it, to be a medievalist. It is to Cambridge, too, that Archbishop Parker, Master of Corpus Christi, belongs, and it is to his college that he left his famous collection of manuscripts. One can only speak with bated breath of the treasures of that library in which Parker concentrated so many of the best and most ancient and rarest materials for medieval history. Beside him stands Sir Robert Cotton, of Jesus, that other prince of manuscript collectors. "If", says Montague James, "these two collections...had been wiped out, the best things in our vernacular literature and the pick of our chronicles would be unknown to us now." But the archbishop was not only a collector, he was an editor of medieval chronicles. If his standards of editorship were deficient in critical instinct and he tampered with his texts, to him are due the *editiones principes* of Gildas and Asser and the St Albans chroniclers. He was a pioneer in the publication of the sources of medieval history, which has gone on, and continually grown in completeness, in meticulous accuracy, and in equipment, till our own day. He may claim to be one of those who have made medieval studies possible.

Less connected with Cambridge than Parker —yet he was an *alumnus* of Trinity—was Sir Henry Spelman, who collected and printed the Councils of the English Church before the Conquest. Here again we are in the region of the publication of sources, documentary in this case, and still more of the work of making them intelligible, for Spelman's *Archaeologus* was a glossary of the obscure law terms of which documents and chronicles were full. Both Spelman's Councils and Glossary of course have long been obsolete: even the *Concilia* of Wilkins, the Prussian scholar who a hundred years later was Lord Almoner's Professor of Arabic, has been superseded in part by Haddan and Stubbs's work for many years, and will be wholly so at not too distant a date. None the less both mark epochs in the study of medieval history.

I can only allude to the work of Fuller of Queens' College. Vivid in his homely realism, he gave us history built largely on contemporary evidence, the *Holie Warre* of the Crusades, the *Church History of Britain*, the *Worthies of England*, and a history of the University itself. He set out to compile, to retell, and to digest a narrative of events. There is something of the primitive about him, for, himself a frank and utter partisan, he humanly felt the scenes he describes—a thing which so few of us can do— the only recipe to make the dry bones live.

But Fuller with his books has long joined his own Worthies. We go to him now, some- times for literary pleasure, sometimes as a source for facts or thoughts of his own century, not as a teacher for earlier times. A smaller man, who accomplished for medieval history a much greater and more enduring work, is Thomas Rymer, of Sidney Sussex. It is super- fluous to insist on the merits of the monu- mental *Foedera*; that collection of documents meets one in countless notes of countless books and articles. If he was not, strictly speaking, a pioneer, he brought to light and made usable a whole department of one of the richest archives of Europe. No doubt his texts are not free from errors; fortunately for his successors, he did not sweep the archives clean of the class of documents he published. But with the *Foedera*, as with the *Concilia*, the medievalist obtained one of the most useful tools in the second division of his sources, the documentary, perhaps now the most fruitful material for new work and new discoveries.

Beside Rymer and Fuller there stands another collector and editor of manuscripts and biographic historian, Henry Wharton of Gonville and Caius College; in Stubbs's words "this wonderful man died...at the age of thirty, having done for the elucidation of English Church History...more than any one before or since". We still use texts published in his *Anglia Sacra*. To publish, however, and even to explain and narrate is not necessarily to interpret, and to reach interpreters of medieval history who are near enough to us to produce answering thoughts, and who do not translate, so to say, from one dead language into another, we must come down to the nineteenth century. In that nearer time should be commemorated two authors, exact contemporaries, now too little read, Samuel Roffey Maitland of St John's and Trinity, and Thomas Greenwood of St John's. Both deserved, first and foremost, the epithet of scholarly. They went back to the sources, they constructed afresh and for themselves from the sources, and discarded the facile repetition of earlier views which so easily becomes a parody or a fiction. Greenwood may be described, perhaps, as a Gibbon *manqué*. Too much of the dignity of history told by the superior person appears in his pompous, rotund periods and in his austere judgement of the Popes. None the less his *Cathedra Petri*, the *History of the Great Latin Patriarchate*, is still profitable to consult. Maitland, the more familiar, is still a storehouse of authentic anecdote and still interesting for his lively controversy and ready learning. He rescued for English readers the Dark Ages from contempt and oblivion.

It is hard to appreciate rightly more recent figures, who have really formed the existing Cambridge school of medieval history, although they were not only bred at Cambridge but taught there. For they did not limit themselves to the Middle Ages. Cunningham, a true pioneer, was an economic historian who took the Middle Ages in his stride. Frederick Maitland, our greatest indigenous name, was a lawyer. Yet the one penetrated deep into the social fabric and material conditions which were the mould of medieval life, and the other with his brilliant imagination made both law and history a study of the human mind and of human nature with their powers and their vagaries. The driest detail took life and colour from his pen, and somehow, while long-dead thoughts and a past environment became sympathetic, intelligible, and clear, Maitland himself, with his wit, his wisdom, his insight and learning, is always before the reader, like the sunlight in a landscape. There is no vain attempt of the author to confuse himself with his theme, nor does the hoarse bass of an older time shrill to us mildly in a modern treble.

Last of all, I may perhaps mention Corbett, for here again the *genius loci* seems evident, the ideal of history based on the sources by critical investigation, each problem considered slowly, thoroughly, independently, afresh, yet with full knowledge of former solutions. That power to keep the mind and judgement free amid the plethora of learning is given to few. In his too scanty monographs Corbett attained it.

There is something non-committal in the title given to the period of European history which these scholars studied: *Medium Aevum*, the Middle Age which lies between Antiquity and the Modern Age in which we live. The name, so far as so colourless a phrase can suggest anything, presupposes more of those other ages than of itself: on the one hand the triumphant Renaissance, the expansion of the world, the discovery and the subjection of the forces of Nature, the growing rationalization of thought, of society, and of government; on the other the dead civilization, still luminous like its marbles, of Greece and Rome, which had crumbled and been submerged in barbarism, yet whose relics were the teachers and inspirers of the intellectual advance of modern Europe. The Middle Age would seem to be the uninhabited, featureless heath dividing from one another ancient tribes cantoned in their tilth and pasture.

It has been the task of medievalists to substitute for this impression of nullity a very different picture, and to give reasons for their faith in the importance and absorbing interest of their study. First of all, to take the humblest defence, they may stress the part played by continuity in the understanding of history. The story of mankind will hardly be rightly conceived if it is known as a succession of disconnected, if brilliant, scenes, separated by blank darkness. True, we do see a decline, which is nearly a collapse, of civilization in Western Europe when the Roman Empire dissolves. But, even if we for the moment disregard the continuance of Antiquity, all important both then and in the future, in the Roman East of Byzantium, yet some part of Rome's ideas and cultural heritage, at the lowest reckoning, lived on and were part of the medieval elements out of which was formed the modern world. Morbid, decaying conditions, too, throw lights on the characteristics of the original healthy organism. We can learn an indispensable something of how to interpret the life of the Roman Empire, its strength and its weakness, from, so to say, an autopsy of its corpse. In like manner, to invade the Modern World at the Renaissance will hardly allow us to understand the first three centuries at least of its evolution: it can only be truly seen in the light of medieval conditions and spiritual performance, which were slowly passing away or rather being transmuted into modern successors. Modern civilization, with its thoughts and aptitudes and all that they imply, did not spout forth suddenly in the sixteenth century, charged with imprisoned gases, like a new geyser from a subterranean cavern. It was the natural inheritor of the preceding age, rich with its accumulated gains, and moulded by its experience. In fact, the separation of modern and medieval is, as we all know, largely artificial. To make it, we have to hew through the living, growing tissues, to break the vitally linked series of events, and to divide the seamless web which is still lengthening before our eyes. It is with peoples as with individuals. We cannot know the real make-up of the mature man without a knowledge of the experiences and tendencies of his childhood and youth. The character then displayed and engrained, the problems he had then to face dominate in some degree his later life.

From this point of view the study of medieval history is an essential concomitant of that of modern history. We cannot understand, for instance, the nature of Tudor rule and the character of the English parliament without tracing the development and the fortunes of an earlier time, or the absolutism of Louis XIV without a reference to Philip the Fair and Louis XI, in fact to earlier monarchs too and their subjects, who left their indelible mark on later Frenchmen. Historic truth, in short, like other truth, is to be sought in the whole, or in as wide stretches as we can get of it, rather than confined in isolated sections, however exact and penetrating the research into them may be.

This view by itself, while it upholds the utility and importance of medieval history, supplies a motive for its study which may seem unduly austere, making it an unavoidable and stony path to a desired goal. But it is not only a dour necessity which impels the medievalist to his study; it is the vivid attraction of the Middle Age itself. He is not called upon to peer into a monotonous twilight wherein actions and thoughts repeat themselves from decade to decade in endless imitation and identity. There was no torpor about the men of the Middle Ages: the happiness of nations without history did not afflict them. For the times were full of new things and of change: they were creative and experimental in every possible way, in law and government, and in the ethos and organization of society, in the range and character of human intercourse, in economic methods and conditions, in that most conservative occupation, agriculture, in thought and theory, in warfare and seafaring, in building and all the

tangible dreams of art, and, if there most un-
consciously, in the very languages that were
spoken, in which we can see the speeches of
modern Europe acquiring the subtlety and
precision which has made them more than a
tool—a light to the intellect. It is only when
we compare the Middle Ages on the one hand
with the rapid transitions of modernity, and on
the other with the varied conceptions of life
and the world which took the place of their
fundamental beliefs, that the medievals give
the impression of fixity. Our descendants,
seeing that our variety proceeds from an
acceptance of certain dominating ideas, may
tax us too, when we have become remote and
obsolete, with sameness. The Middle Ages
developed under prepossessions of religious
authority and of an eternal order for mankind,
in an ethos of emotional indiscipline, and in
material conditions of subjection to the soil
with its produce and its geography. These three
limitations gave a character to them, which for
long kept them within a habitation that became
too narrow. A slow movement towards

liberation from that engrossing authority and conviction, a slow growth in self-control, a slow creation of wealth and power apart from the soil, a slow triumph over mere distance, over marsh and wood and mountain, were among the achievements of medieval man and were causes of the transition to modern times.

In fact, within the limitations just suggested, the immobile Middle Ages on closer acquaintance resolve themselves into a shifting scene, a scene too which has a consistent development and creativeness, even if, as in all developments, there are in it false starts and barren inventions. To take, for instance, the field of law, we find barbaric customs first set side by side with degenerate Roman Law, the era of so-called personal law; we see in some lands tribal law going through an evolution of its own; in other, Latin lands, the two elements blend and change into a composite, local, territorial custom. We find this product altering and advancing under the influence of new needs and under the tutelage of the renewed study of the *Corpus Iuris Civilis* of Justinian. And the advance is intentional, the work of lawyers and judges, sometimes of statesmen. There is a will to live by law. Beside it there is the expanding *Corpus* of the Canon Law, both a register and a cause of growing civilization; the canonical jurisprudence is the creation of successive generations of lawyer popes, of the canonists of the Roman Curia and Bologna, of administrator bishops. Not utterly dissimilar in the secular sphere is the English Common Law, where the creative instinct has likewise full play, whatever it may derive from blended customs and from hints from Roman and canonical jurisprudence. In a general lecture one must name rather than describe—a fortunate circumstance for the ill-informed lecturer —but the mere mention is enough to suggest that process of development and creation, of the decay which is new birth, in a word, of that incessant progress in the art of life which the history of medieval law shrouds and reveals.

The same fact stands out as clearly if we look at the method and extent of government from the Dark Ages onward. We start with barbaric tribes taking over the shattered fabric of Roman government. At first, tribal loyalty to a semi-divine race of kings—an immense asset in tribal durability—on the one side and the habit of obedience to the State on the other produce a simulacrum of Roman order: Merovingian kings appear—if they only appear—to govern in some sort like their imperial predecessors. But the little glimmer of Romanism that flickers on becomes less and less, and facts of existing life tell more and more. Distant government can only be carried on by the lords of land with their local wealth, the land, and their local adherents. Charlemagne, an omni-present hero of genius, may delay the change and hide the fact, but in the end the subject will obey the local lord who can help or harm rather than the far-off king who can only inter-vene at long last and then probably through the very men who have become local dynasts, not functionaries. It is the genesis, or part of the genesis—for that has its military, not governmental side—of feudalism. I will not enter into the fray to discuss the strict definition of feudalism or at what moment it may be declared indubitably in being. That system— if we may call it a system—arose in France under the pressure of certain historic needs and events, among which the invasions of the Northmen are conspicuous. It spread, partly by imitation, partly by force, in varying forms and composition into other lands, well prepared for it by their previous home-grown needs and circumstances, which none the less might not ever have produced feudalism if left to their own devices. The result, however, was that feudalism became the method of government for a great part of Europe. The vassal lord, supported in turn by his vassals, was governor and judge of his lands which he held not in plain ownership but conditionally on terms of feudal loyalty with feudal duties including military service. The king was the perpetual source of government and of landed wealth. But his exercise of government was intermittent save in the lands which, with their wealth, he retained in his own hands.

But feudalism is barely crystallized before

a new monarchic change begins. Feudalism assumed a monarch, vassalage meant onerous duties to a lord. Cessation from invasion, the very systematization of the feudal structure itself, the efforts of the Church, the Crusades— an escape-valve for warlike ardour—all produced an embryo order and minimum of security which allowed wealth and civilization to increase, and favoured the wealth-making classes, farmers and merchants, who wished for more peace and more rational government. So the kings have their chance, or where they have not, the greater lords of wide lands have theirs. This monarchy is feudal; it rests largely on feudal rights and methods; it derives great part of its strength—not all—from feudal law and feudal ideas. It must do so, for landed wealth and resources are still the chief form of economic power, and land-owning is still feudal in nature. But with the old a still older element creeps back into government, the bureaucracy that, at first more than half feudal, will replace feudalism. The royal employee, the servant of the central government and its master, fortified by landed wealth, served by commercial wealth which multiplies under royal protection, is on the way to be stronger than the local lord. Inspired by the traditional awe and sanctity which attach to the anointed king set up by God to give peace and justice, he overruns the Western realms. The will to obey, the dread of the sovereign liege, has grown and become habitual. Distance has come to mean only delay, not inhibition. An orderly structure of administration, responding to the central impulse, has re-arisen in Europe in the close of the Middle Ages.

There is no need to say how partial and over-simplified is this picture. I have left out the rise of Estates and the doctrine of consent, the right to decree and to tax, the model of the Church, which, however feudalized, was based on, and was permeated to the core by, other motives and other forces. I only give this selective evolution as one of the greatest examples of medieval inventiveness. Even as such, it is a syncopated sketch of a ceaseless activity in devices and methods and experiments, an endless diversity in which nothing is standardized, where no institution remains unaltered for long. They share the inexhaustible novelty and succession of Nature itself.

Feudalism and centralizing monarchy were only two among the expedients devised in the Middle Ages for the work of government. The University in which we live tells us of another system then brought into being: that of free association. For the medieval universities, governed by assemblies of their members and by officials elected by them, are an instance of the same kind of contrivance as the chartered town or the commune. In both men formed new ties, new governmental authorities, by common consent, and appointed directly or indirectly their own executive. The bewildering complexity of councils, societies, boards, and officers which we encounter in an Italian commune, for instance, is a testimony to the slow and piecemeal effort by which this mechanism was built up. New functions to be assumed, rival claims to power to be liquidated, new problems to be solved, all left their mark on the structure. It was a successful attempt of laymen, independent of earlier sanctions and traditional machinery, to take over the task which kings and feudal barons and the ecclesiastical hierarchy had performed—and it did not stop at replacement: it provided, however clumsily, for the arising needs of a non-feudal, highly commercial and industrial, bourgeois society. It was, then, a new form of liberty, a contrivance for men to act in concert by some form of corporate action. True that this innovating effort came sooner or later to the end of its tether: it led, as times changed, to a blind alley incapable of further progress. The self-governing town ended either in tyranny or in so close an oligarchy as to dispense with that wide collective action of many in common government with which it had begun. None the less the experiment bears witness to the extraordinary creativeness of the Middle Age and the originality of the conceptions then discovered. They were spiritual, not only practical triumphs, the workings of the human mind to subdue its circumstances and its own defects.

Wherever we turn there is the same change and inventiveness. Whether it is the development of armour in warfare, or of new weapons and tactics, of the sailing ship, of cathedral, castle, and dwelling house, of dyeing and dressing cloth, of banking and bills of exchange in commerce, we find the same continual search for more knowledge, for better methods, for more adequate human life. Greed, egoism, and mere reaction to external pressure play their part in the process, but there is something else: the desire to live by law and reason, not only by scanty custom and traditions, becoming a misfit, and inherited awe.

It is not by idealizing medieval times as a golden age of stability and faith that we best perceive their greatness. The endeavour of men of that age, we may say, and their true praise, was to escape from themselves, from conditions which they were well aware were evil. It is true that they looked on it not in modern terms of progress but as an attempt to return to an idealized past, as efforts to remedy sin and decay. The imagined reaction and repair were none the less advance. In this endeavour they did marvels, and as marvels are often done, they not infrequently did them in vain, or at least without the reward of lasting success. But one vast cause of failure, or of very insufficient achievement, is perhaps also one source of the charm of the Middle Ages to the student to-day. I have referred to the limitation imposed on them by the undisciplined emotions of the men of those days. For the very lack of self-control, the naïve, unreflecting display of natural character and surrender to impulse and emotion good or bad, that childlike response to outer stimulus or inner passion in grown men, often of unsurpassed mental powers, allows the vivid appearance of the inborn variety of mankind. Love and hate, mingling like the colours of shot silk, truth and treachery, greed, ambition and self-abnegation, wrath and relenting, cruelty and mercy, pride and fawning, tyranny and justice, skill, craft, stupidity, succeed to, mix with, and contrast with one another in unrestrained violence. How these natural im-

(28)

pulses break out in the early Crusades: the passionate, if elementary and almost primitive, devotion, spreading by mass-infection in a rude society, the adventurousness, the hatred of the unknown infidel, the dreams of ambition and crass greed of fabulous wealth! How straightforward heroism and loyalty, brigand-like ferocity and licence, shrewd generalship, wild disarray, and brainless ignorance clash and combine! How petty rivalry and vanity, reckless schemes, and cool statesmanship stand out in glaring colours, and exist, untrammelled by self-consciousness, in the same man!

Then again, how like in this frank, un-thinking self-revelation, if nothing else, are Henry II of England and St Francis! The rest-less Henry, with his lusts and rages, with the crude egoism of his forest-law, with his violent and constant affections, is yet the hard-headed ruler, gifted with a capacity for thinking out practical methods and regulations which are the fount of law rather than law itself. He is conscious of his kingly mission, he aims to fulfil it ambitiously, he will show business-like moderation when untempted, or essentially short-sighted cunning when his greed is aroused as in the seizure of the Vexin, or a simple instinct of feudal duty when he retires from Toulouse before his suzerain in person; or again he will writhe cursing in the straw when balked and provoked by Becket. There is spontaneity here as there is in St Francis. That character has been dilated upon too often and too long, it shines out too realistically from the words of his contemporaries who were in touch with his present self and the immediate impression of him to encourage now another estimate, cut, dried, and lifeless. But one may yet recall here the inner harmony of St Francis which makes the life of this poet itself a poem. From the decisive moment when, weak from his illness, he saw the landscape of Assisi, "But the beauty of the fields, the pleasantness of the vineyards and whatever is fair to see could in no way delight him", through the brief vain dream of excelling chivalry to the bridal with Lady Poverty and until the last scene among the ashes at Portiuncula, all his qualities seem to work together towards one purpose, one personal ideal, supereminent, satisfying, fit for him, that way of life which he sought and discovered for himself in the Gospel and did not borrow from the great ascetics of the past. His, if any one's, was the path of self-expression. He "saw one clue to life and followed it".

Characters and scenes crowd thick and fast in the age of Dante. The Florentine chiefs, with their burning rivalries, the wise and sly Matteo Visconti, the pain-racked, bullying Boniface VIII, the venomous Nogaret, the stolid Philip the Fair, Dante himself, outlive the generations. Later again, we can watch those contemporaries, at one end of Europe the brothers Pedro the Cruel and Henry of Trastamara grappling like wild beasts, eager for murder, in the tent of Bertrand du Guesclin on Don Quixote's plain of Montiel, and at the other the neurotic patriot king and shabbiest of diplomats, Charles of Bohemia and Luxemburg, whittling away a stick with restless fingers, scanning his company with ever-shifty eyes, scanning all of them except the prosy envoy who spoke in embarrassed neglect before him, and who was then amazed when the emperor took up and answered his oration point by point.

It is easy in this coming and going of personalities, now humdrum, now bizarre, but always untamed, to slip into the picturesque and superficial. Yet there is a real knowledge to be gained in their study. These people in their foibles, their motives, and their passions, lay themselves bare in a genuine way in which few men of more mature times would wish or even be able to do. Only from the abnormal and unbalanced could you now expect such revelations, which in their nature would be untrustworthy and erratic. But medieval men were not breaking through habitual restraint or thrusting behind them a long array of second thoughts and provident cautions. They were nearer than we to the springs of action, those simpler, stronger traits of human nature which draw the lesser and complex after them like the eddies in a cataract. We see in them more clearly in a kind of nakedness the primary needs and factors which decide the main course of history. In them we can discern the stretch of the tugging muscles and the throb of the pulses with the skin removed.

"Grief and joy and hope and fear
Play their pageants everywhere."

They may help us to guess at the present and future if not to make vain prophecies of the unknown.

Thus there is a manifold charm to draw us to the study of the Middle Ages. There is their creativeness to which we moderns are so much indebted. Then "grew the arts of war and peace". They brought Western Europe out of barbarism to civilization. There is also—and here we embark on a new theme—the sheer excellence of many of their creations in themselves: their thought massive and subtle, their building beautiful beyond words that speaks none the less a universal tongue, their literature which still sounds the chords of the heart as it did once in men so strange and rude so long ago. "The iniquity of oblivion" has there not yet scattered "her poppy".

The opinion may be ventured that the more excellent of these creations are marked by and owe their specific quality to the lack of self-consciousness which, I have suggested, was generally characteristic of medieval men. It is not so much lack of art and science in doing things, but that the motives for doing them are frank and spontaneous, unclogged by philosophic detachment or inner conflict of aims. The Icelandic sagaman's aim is to tell a traditional tale of real people fully, vividly, and precisely. His revelation—not so much delineation—of character is all the more true and penetrating because he has no wish to show expertness in psychology or to concoct a marvellous plot, full of nature, art, and poetic justice. Rather, he would have been bewildered by psychological analysis, and his audience would have resented an intentional disturbance of the traditional sequence of events. He had no by-ends, save the eternal by-end of making a living and pleasing the hearers, which was only to be served by telling the story well. The object of the legislators of a commune was not blurred by thoughts of a perfect philosophic constitution on first principles to turn it from the primary need of a working machine which should combine certain obvious interests and exclude certain others. Their aim in this resembled that of the builder of a sailing ship: to construct something to float, to be steerable, to be swift and stable. It was eminently practical. In the same manner and with more splendid results worked the builders of cathedral and abbey. First of all, they had to provide for the uses of the cult— the mass, the processions, and the hours, and the watching throng; it must express the awe, the veneration of the Domus Dei—then they could contrive how to make these spaces, whether open or withdrawn from uninitiated approach, more light, more adorned, more vocal with glass or painting. It was the advance of engineering skill which allowed and produced the Gothic edifice, an increasing knowledge of technique applied towards the direct, practical purposes of religion. As virtuosity creeps in we move away from this simplicity of aim. The builder or the artist becomes more self-conscious in his own make-up, more profound and far more wide in outlook; and he is aware of it. He has gained a volume of thought and skill, and he presents it to a world that sees what he is doing with a critic's eye. It is, I still believe, a wiser, freer, riper age that does these newer, humaner things in the Renaissance and after; but it has lost that youthful, single-minded charm of the Middle Ages, or, more truly, has exchanged it for a fascination of its own. *Don Quixote* in 1600 will give us a picture of an age and people, a meditative self-knowledge and contemplation of human nature and human vicissitudes which may move us as Cervantes willed, but it does not give us the artless charm, childlike in its elderliness, of *Aucassin and Nicolette* told just to please by the "first-endeavouring tongue" of the "vieil caitif", told to a world that, as a whole, did not concentrate on probability and reasonableness, that was not yet garbed in sophisticated habit and not yet mature.

Further, we can, I think, see more clearly the larger, more sweeping movements of history in the Middle Ages than in modern times. For one thing, much of those medieval movements have reached their close. We can see whither the tide was tending, we can watch the changing shape of the wave as it gathers height and force and swells to its breaking; its lesser crests and indentations need not obsess us and make us lose the general contour and direction. And the very distance of the events we regard gives us something of the same advantage. We can perceive the scene into which they fit and their right proportion. In the midst of the Alps the nearer peaks obscure the range; even at an altitude the mountains may rise round you bewilderingly like a tumultuous sea. But, somewhat removed at Monte Generoso, the whole barrier range spreads before you in its geographical shape east and west, the snow-bound and the lesser members ranged in order in a system; and on the south there lies the Lombard plain like a map, blotted with its red cities, seamed with its silver rivers, bounded by its southern frontier, the blue-grey Apennines. You see the structure of the land. This pleasure in proportion and perspective undisguised by

(37)

pettier accidents and near obstacles, unharassed by the hope or fear of the invisible event, is given by the far-off evolution of medieval history.

But for such an effect our study of the Middle Ages must not be restricted to one couple of centuries or country, however much our particular interest must necessarily be focussed on a special subject, land, or period. We must see the panorama, although we concentrate on one or other of its parts. Here we may recognise one of the advantages and one of the duties of a flourishing school of medievalists such as Cambridge possesses. Members of such a school have the opportunity between them of covering the ground. Ecclesiastical, literary, economic, administrative, and constitutional specialists, experts in French or German or Italian or other foreign history, should exist and be trained here. The more diverse and far afield their range of study, the more we are saved from parochialism in history—that prison of learning—the more fruitful and educative our discipline may be. The meaning of history is largely a matter of comparison. The France of Philip the Fair and the England of Edward I throw mutual light on each other; the organization of the Church illuminates the royal bureaucracies and their methods; the fortunes of Lombard, Visigothic, and Frankish kings are each clearer if we mark their common features and their divergencies; we can detect the decisive factors which made out of like beginnings such unlike destinies. We deal in that inexhaustible subject, man and his works, and man and his works vary with place and circumstance. We believe that nowhere more than in the period of the Middle Ages are the inter-effects of mankind and the environment which it inherits and which it shapes—an environment both mental and material—more clearly shown. For that knowledge we need the labours of many to glean in the multiple diversities of so wide a field. And the more varied their experience the richer our knowledge, the fuller our understanding will be of a time of whose gains we are inheritors, and which has so much to tell us of the workings, the triumphs, and the failures of the human mind.

9 781107 644625